BEGINNER'S GUIDE TO PUBLISHING BOOKS

ON

kindle

&

createspace

SARCO PRESS

ISBN-13: 978-1515129738

ISBN-10: 151512973X

http://sarcopress.com

"Every writer needs a professional like sarco2000. He does precise, professional quality work. He is the best I have found, and I will be including him in a blog post."

- Customer

"I needed complete help with formatting for CreateSpace, and this seller did everything I wanted and more. If I needed some changes, he did them. He was very responsive to all my request. I would recommend this seller to everyone. He's kind and very quick to respond. Five stars for him. Thanks!"

- Customer

"He did a great job! As a publisher, I appreciate the good work. He met all my expectations. I will do business with him regularly. I highly recommend this gig! Thank you :-)"

- Customer

"I definitely recommend this gig! He is a real professional. Communication is excellent and the service is fast and efficient. Thank you :-)"

- Customer

"He went above and beyond what was expected in this order, I would highly recommend and will use your services again!"

- Customer

Contents

About This Book

I am the owner of Sarco Press, a company which formats books for Createspace and Kindle. I enjoy spending my days building beautiful books from rough-looking manuscripts. My clients are always pleased, but sometimes they need help after the formatting process is completed.

And then there is Scratch.

A few months ago I was helping my friend Scratch to get his book published on Amazon Kindle. I gave very specific instructions on what to do. Despite this, my friend nearly gave up in exasperation, calling the Kindle publishing process "The Amazon Maze".

Scratch is skilled in writing and storytelling, but computers and the internet are not areas where he has a lot of experience. Scratch grew up in a different age - he can type a book in Word, but formatting it and publishing it were great hurdles for him to overcome. I formatted his book for him, but that was only half the battle. Getting the book published was a whole new challenge for him.

My friend Scratch is the inspiration for writing this book. Scratch is an awesome storyteller, and his stories need to be told.

I realized that there must be millions of authors out there who have a great manuscript but who are unwilling or unable to follow the next step--getting the book published. So I wrote this book to help authors get their stories published. I want to explain in very simple terms (with a lot of images) what self-published authors need to know to push their books through the publishing process.

This book is not a formatting guide. I am writing a book about formatting for Createspace or Kindle using free and opensource software and it will have even more pictures than this one. This book is a publishing guide. Publishing should only come after proofreading/editing and formatting.

Here are the five steps to the process of writing and publishing a book:

1) Write the book
2) Have the manuscript proofread and edited

3) Format the book for Kindle and Createspace

4) Make covers or pay someone to make covers

5) Publish the book on Kindle and Createspace

If you're reading this book, you have completed tasks 1-4, and are now ready to publish.

Don't worry! Publishing is the easiest part of the whole process!

What is Book Formatting?

The Author's task is to write the story. The Book Formatter's job is to put the story in a standard (and sometimes creative) format recognizable to the industry and to readers. If there is a mistake in the print book or ebook design, a reader will feel that something is wrong. This can lead to a subconscious decision that the book production is amateurish or self-published, and may influence the reader's opinion of the content of the book.

Sometimes the author and the book formatter are the same person. Often the author is too busy writing books, and will hire an outside party to format.

Print Books

An experienced print Book Formatter will organize the front matter, the body, and the back matter. Sections of the book will begin on the recto, or right hand side, of the book. Front matter is numbered differently from the body. Headers, footers, chapter headings, drop caps, formatting of graphics, tables, bullet lists, recto formatting and tables of contents are all handled by the Book Formatter.

A good Book Formatter will be comfortable with the mechanics of book design, yet be receptive to the requirements of the author. Authors may have a style in mind for the print book and the Book Formatter's job is to help get the idea across to the reader using existing standards as guidelines. Good communication between the author and the Book Formatter is essential!

EBooks

Formatting ebooks is a little different. An experienced ebook Formatter will format in a way that offers the best presentation on a variety of reading devices. There are millions of reading devices in reader's hands, and each user has their own font settings and line space settings. Ebook formatting must be kept simple; there is less room for creativity when formatting.

Finally, a Book Formatter may guide the author through the process of getting her book ready for Createspace or ebook publishing.

What is Publishing?

Publishing is the process of issuing books for sale. Most self-published authors use Kindle and Createspace to perform that task.

Createspace is a company which is owned by Amazon. The Createspace platform provides a way for Amazon authors to publish paperback versions of their books.

It is important to note that publishing your books on Kindle or Createspace does not mean that Amazon owns the rights to your book. Your book is your own intellectual property and belongs to you, as stated on your copyright page.

Speaking of copyrights, just inserting your copyright into your book page should be good enough to ensure your work isn't stolen by someone else. However, it is possible to strengthen your claim to the rights of your book by registering your copyright with the US Copyright Office at http://www.copyright.gov/. The cost at this time is $35 and it takes about a month.

More information about how to copyright a book can be found here: http://www.wikihow.com/Copyright-a-Book

Thanks to my author friend Michael Rusin for the information about copyrights.

Proofreading, Previewing & Proofing

There is a difference between Previewing, Proofing, and Proofreading, and some authors get them confused.

Proofreading should be done before your book is formatted and sent to Createspace or Kindle. The point of ordering a Createspace "proof" is to check for printing errors or formatting errors--NOT to check for typos and grammar mistakes! Typos, grammar and spelling should be taken care of before you get to publishing!

Previewing is the act of visually checking your formatted book before it is published on Kindle or Createspace. Sometimes text or images don't line up with the margins, or the formatting may have introduced a typo.

Proofing in this book is used to mean ordering a physical paperback copy from Createspace to check for printing errors or formatting errors. In the context of Kindle, it could mean buying your Kindle book to read on your Kindle device and check for errors.

Previewing Your Createspace Book

After formatting the book, the Book Formatter will produce a PDF file ready for upload to Createspace. The uploadable file will be in Portable Document Format (PDF). The author should review the PDF file before uploading to Createspace. For this job some authors use Adobe Acrobat Reader DC, but there are other free options available. For quick PDF viewing without installing a large program, I find that Foxit Reader is my go-to favorite. It's light and fast and doesn't take up hundreds of megabytes of hard drive space like Adobe's bloated Acrobat.

The author should check for errors and offer input to the Book Formatter for any changes requested. With my Book Formatting jobs I usually offer free unlimited formatting revisions, so the author can relax knowing she is not under a time constraint to get the formatting correct. But I understand that authors want to get their work published as soon as possible. I try to answer all requests within a few hours at most.

After the job has been completed, the author and the book formatter may continue to edit the file, up until the author has ordered and received a physical book from Createspace, proofed it and is satisfied!

Kindle Books Need Simple Formatting!

First, it is important to realize that **Kindle books shouldn't have complicated formatting**! Things need to be kept simple so that the book will be readable on the thousands of different devices in the hands of people. And each person has his or her device set up with personal font settings and line spacings. So if we try to add small caps to a Kindle book, it may look great on one person's device, but it may look terrible on another person's device!

The same goes for graphics formatting on Kindle books. All images should be centered in the screen and sized so that they will be readable on everything from an iPhone to a 10" Android tablet. And trying to wrap text around images is asking for trouble!

Previewing Your Kindle Book

I highly recommend downloading and installing Kindle Previewer. It is an Amazon tool that professional authors and formatters use to check their Kindle books before they upload them (and it is also what I use). It will convert the file to a MOBI format and then provide a window with a WYSIWYG presentation of how the Kindle book will look on various devices.

Short of side-loading a MOBI file to an actual Kindle device, Kindle Previewer or the Online Previewer will provide the most accurate presentation of the ebook on various devices. Make sure to check various devices by working the "Devices" button in the menu at the top in the screenshot below.

When you're done previewing the ebook, either recommend changes to the formatter or, if you think its good to go, upload it to Kindle Direct Publishing (KDP).

How to Download and Install Kindle Previewer

There is a complete user guide here:

kindlepreviewer.s3.amazonaws.com/UserGuide.pdf

Download and install the previewer from Amazon: http://www.amazon.com/gp/feature.html?docId=1000765261

After installation, on my Windows PC, the new program shows up in START MENU --> ALL PROGRAMS --> AMAZON --> KINDLE PREVEIWER

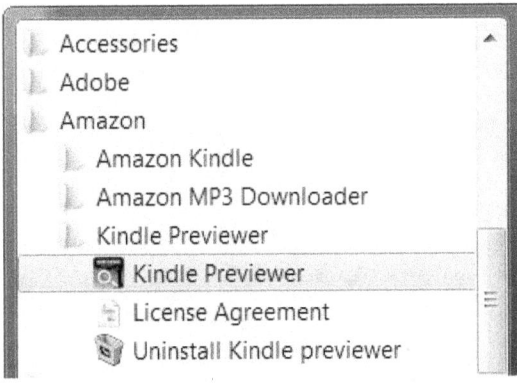

Start the program, then go to FILE --> OPEN BOOK and browse to the directory where the EPUB file is located. Alternatively, you may be able to simple double-click the epub file to open it.

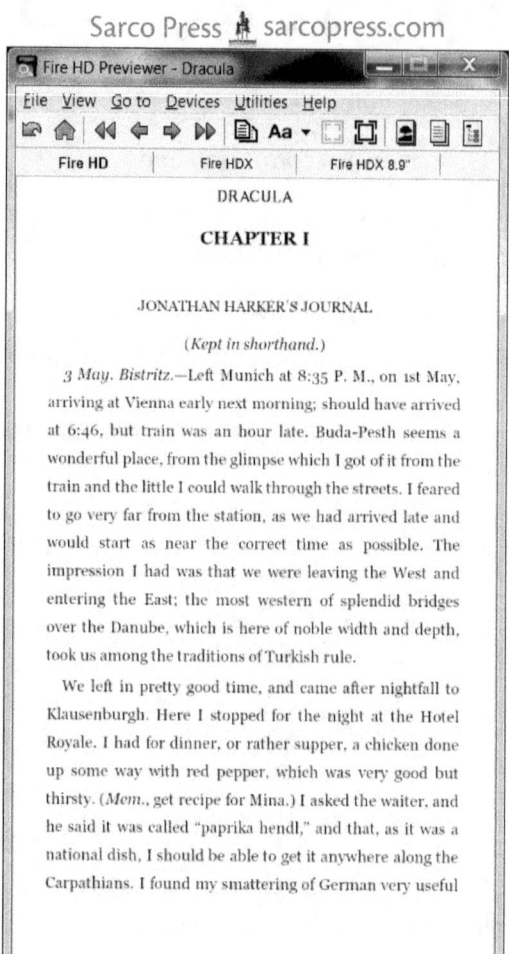

The Kindle Previewer program will convert the file to MOBI format, then give you an option to see where the new MOBI file is located, and/or if you choose it will open the MOBI file. Then you can see what the book looks like on a kindle.

Play with the DEVICES menu button to see what the book looks like on various kindle devices. Don't forget to check different device screen sizes and also try the e-ink devices.

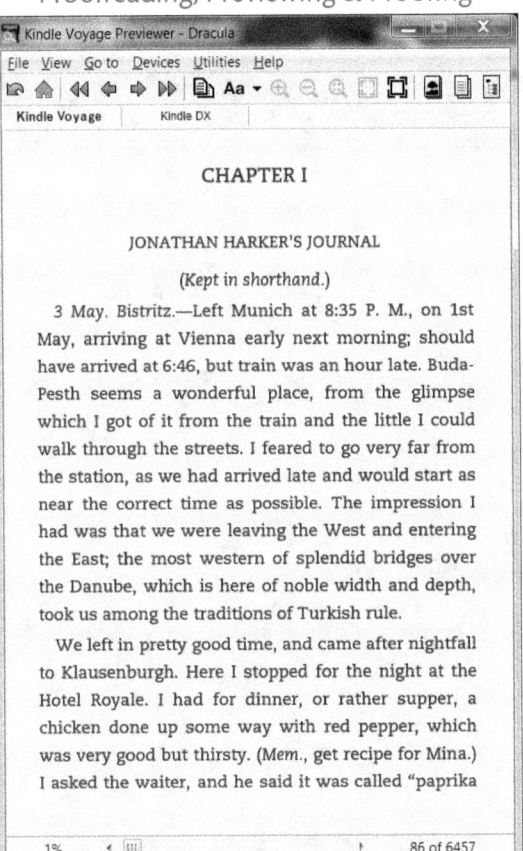

And check the NCX Table of Contents:

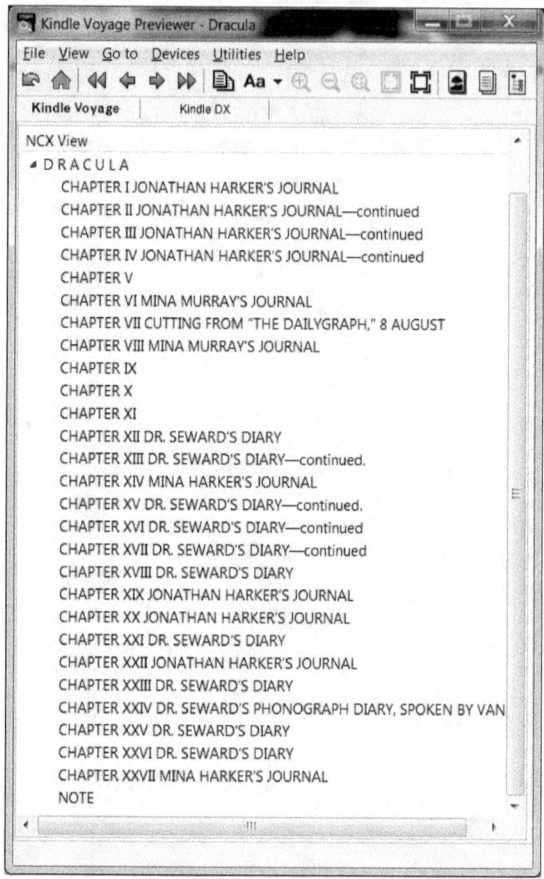

There is another way to preview your book

You can also simply upload your book to KDP and look at the online previewer.

Instructions for getting to the Online Previewer will be in the Step-by-Step Guide later in the book.

Section One: Kindle

Why Publish Books On Kindle?

The answer is obvious: Amazon Kindle has the largest market share of potential readers! If your book is on Amazon it will be available to millions of readers. And iPad and Android users won't be left out: the Kindle app is available for Apple and Android devices, meaning those readers can buy and download your book to read on their non-Kindle devices.

If you are only going to publish on one ebook platform, it should be Kindle.

And the Kindle publishing process is ridiculously easy. As long as you have a well written and well-formatted book, the process is quite painless.

The Bare Minimum You Should Know About Kindle Publishing

EPUB is the format that many authors use to upload their Kindle books to KDP. KDP also accepts Word documents or MOBI files. If you upload a Word document, you can't trust that Amazon will format it the way you would like it. It is easier to control the formatting if you upload a version of your book that is already in EPUB format.

I make the epubs in either Word or InDesign, and tweak them in another program afterward. If you ever really feel like you need to edit the EPUB later, you can download and use Sigil. There is a learning curve, just as there is with MS Word.

Another good reason to have an EPUB file is that you can use it to upload your book to other book distributors like Smashwords if you feel like you can reach more readers that way.

If you think your book might need changes in the text, make sure it's done before sending it to the Book Formatter! Some formatters will make author changes during the formatting process or even after the job is complete, but some won't. And even if they are willing to make changes, they may be busy working on other books and will get to your changes when they have time. If the changes are major, it could affect the formatting of the book, requiring even more work and possibly more money.

Kindle Publishing Overview

This section will outline the parts of the Kindle publishing process

- Kindle Direct Publishing (KDP) account setup
- Tax Information setup
- Bookshelf Steps 1-7 - Title Information
- Bookshelf Steps 8-11 - Rights and Pricing
- Find your Kindle book's Amazon Page
- Find your Kindle book's sales rank

Step By Step Guide to Publishing a Kindle book

Sign In To KDP

First go to kdp.amazon.com to make an account or log into your existing account. An existing Amazon customer account won't work; you'll have to make an account on Kindle Direct Publishing (KDP).

Your email address will be the username, and it can be the same email address you use on your regular Amazon account. BUT you don't have to have a regular Amazon account to have a KDP account, they are completely separate.

Sign In

What is your e-mail or mobile number?

E-mail or mobile number:

Do you have an Amazon.com password?

○ **I am a new customer.**
(you'll create a password later)

◉ **I am a returning customer,**
and my password is:

Sign in using our secure server ▶

Forgot your password?

Creating A New Account

To start a new account, go to kdp.amazon.com and follow these steps:

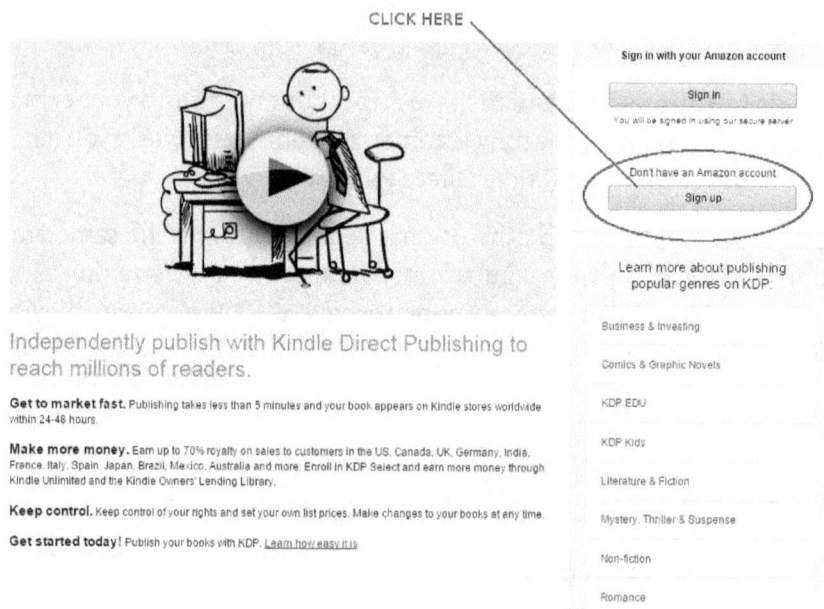

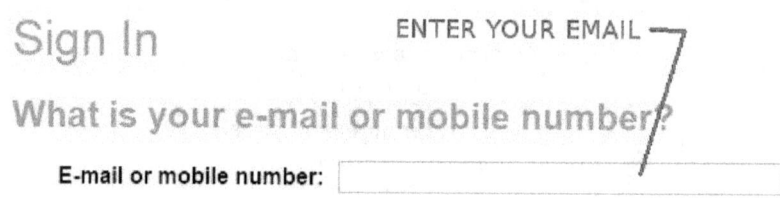

Registration

New to Amazon.com? Register Below.

My name is:

My e-mail address is:

Type it again:

Protect your information with a password

This will be your only Amazon.com password.

Enter a new password:

Type it again:

FILL OUT THE FIELDS,
THEN CLICK HERE

Create account

You will be taken to this page. Click "Agree" at the bottom right.

kindle direct publishing   **Kindle Direct Publishing Terms of Service**

To continue to use the Kindle Direct Publishing, we need you to accept our Terms and Conditions. By clicking **Agree**, you confirm you have read and agree to these Terms and Conditions.

By "list price in any sales channel," we mean the suggested or recommended retail price or, if you sell your book directly to end users, your own sales price, for an edition of the book available outside of our Program.

5. Additional 70% Royalty Option Terms and Conditions

i. Book Eligibility: Books that consist primarily of public domain content are not eligible for the 70% Royalty Option.

ii. Distribution Territory: If you select the 70% Royalty Option for a Digital Book, you must make it available to us for distribution in each territory for which you have appropriate distribution rights, and you must comply with any other restrictions or requirements we may provide from time to time for the 70% Royalty Option in the Program Policies.

iii. New Features: Any new feature incorporated into the Program will apply to all Digital Books distributed under the 70% Option even if we make the feature optional for other Digital Books.

iv. Non-Compliance: If at any time your Digital Book does not meet the requirements for the 70% Royalty Option, the Royalty for the Digital Book will be as provided in the 35% Royalty Option and we can adjust previously reported or paid Royalties based on the 35% Royalty Option.

6. Other Pricing Terms

i. Minimum and Maximum List Prices: To be accepted in the Program, Digital Books must have List Prices within the range of minimum and maximum List Prices indicated here.

Note that if your Digital Book is eligible for the 70% royalty option, your Digital Book will earn 70% on each sale of the Digital Book at a Promotional List Price set under the Kindle MatchBook program or the Kindle Countdown Deals program regardless of whether the Promotional List Price is within the maximum and minimum list price requirements for the 70% royalty option.

ii. Price Matching Determinations : If you notify us through Contact Us (by selecting the topic Pricing & Royalties – Price Matching) that you believe we have made an error in price-matching your Digital Book, we will review the issue and make best efforts to correct the error, if any, going forward as soon as practicable.

View printer friendly version

Agree   Cancel

KDP will take you to this page, where you can fill out your account information by clicking the link:

Fill out the information as shown:

Your Account

After you click the yellow button you'll be taken to the Tax Information Interview. Choose Yes or No in the select box. For purposes of this book, I am choosing "Yes" I am a US citizen.

Tax Information Interview

Getting started

What to expect

This short U.S. tax interview will guide you through a step-by-step process to submit required U.S. tax information to Amazon.

What you will need

- U.S. tax identification number and/or foreign (non-U.S.) income tax identification number, if applicable.

- Printer, if you do not wish to provide an electronic signature.

Note: Only the English alphabet, numbers, and special characters & - , ` / # . % are accepted.

For U.S. tax purposes, are you a U.S. person?

In general, you are considered a U.S. person if you are a (1) U.S. citizen, (2) U.S. resident, or (3) entity organized under the laws of the U.S.

Exit without saving

Save and continue

Then on the next page click where it says "Select One":

Tax Information Interview

You have selected that you are a U.S. person for tax purposes. We will now gather your personal or business information to complete IRS Form W-9.

Taxpayer information

Select your Federal Tax Classification and complete the name and address fields. The "Name" field is required and should be the name of the individual or business that will report the income on a U.S. income tax return. If you are an individual completing the interview on behalf of a business, do not enter your personal name in the "Name" line unless you are completing on behalf of a single-member LLC and you are the individual sole owner.

CLICK HERE

Federal Tax Classification	Select One
Name	
Optional **Business or trade name**	
Address Country	United States
Street address	
Optional **Address 2** Suite, Unit, Building, Floor, etc	
City or town	
State	Select One
ZIP code	

Unless you have a real company and know what you are doing, select "Individual/Sole Proprietor" and fill out the rest of the fields.

Tax Information Interview

You have selected that you are a U.S. person for tax purposes. We will now gather your personal or business information to complete IRS Form W-9.

Taxpayer information

Select your Federal Tax Classification and complete the name and address fields. The "Name" field is required and should be the name of the individual or business that will report the income on a U.S. income tax return. If you are an individual completing the interview on behalf of a business, do not enter your personal name in the "Name" line unless you are completing on behalf of a single-member LLC and you are the individual sole owner.

SELECT THIS

Federal Tax Classification	Individual/sole proprietor
	C Corporation
Name	S Corporation
	Partnership
Optional Business or trade name	Trust/estate
	Limited liability company
Address Country	Other

Street address

Optional Address 2
Suite, Unit, Building, Floor, etc

City or town

State — Select One

ZIP code

FILL OUT THE REST OF THE FIELDS AND CLICK HERE

Exit without saving   Previous   Save and continue

Review:

Tax Information Interview

You have selected that you are a U.S. person for tax purposes. We will
now gather your personal or business information to complete IRS
Form W-9.

MAKE SURE EVERYTHING IS CORRECT

Taxpayer information

Select your Federal Tax Classification and complete the name and address
fields. The "Name" field is required and should be the name of the individual
or business that will report the income on a U.S. income tax return. If you are
an individual completing the interview on behalf of a business, do not enter
your personal name in the "Name" line unless you are completing on behalf of
a single-member LLC and you are the individual sole owner.

Federal Tax Classification	Individual/sole proprietor ⬍
Name	
Optional Business or trade name	
Address Country	United States ⬍
Street address	
Optional Address 2 Suite, Unit, Building, Floor, etc	
City or town	
State	⬍
ZIP code	

Tax identification

Select whether you are providing your Social Security Number (SSN) or
Individual Tax Identification Number (ITIN), or Employer Identification Number
(EIN) as your Tax Identification Number (TIN), then enter the number.

The TIN that you provide must match the "Name" line in the taxpayer
information section. Do not enter the TIN that matches the name you entered
on the "Business or trade name" line, if applicable.

If you are a sole proprietor and you have an EIN, you may enter your EIN or
SSN. If you are a resident alien, enter your ITIN or SSN. If you are a single-
member LLC, enter the owner's SSN or EIN. Do not enter the disregarded
entity's EIN.

MAKE SURE YOUR SSN IS
CORRECT, THEN CLICK
HERE

U.S. TIN Type	⦿ SSN or ITIN ○ EIN
SSN or ITIN Please enter numbers and dashes only Format: XXX-XX-XXXX	

☐ I received my SSN or ITIN within the last 60 days

Exit without saving		Previous	Save and continue

Amazon will verify your name and Social Security Number. If they don't match, you won't be able to proceed.

Your Tax ID is being validated. This may take several seconds.

Then you must review the W9 Tax form. You can't actually click anywhere on this form.

Tax Information Interview

THIS IS FOR REVIEW, YOU CAN'T CLICK ANYTHING HERE!

Review

Review the taxpayer identification form to ensure the accuracy of your previous inputs. If any fields are not correct, please go back to the relevant screen and update your information.

Form **W-9**
(Rev. August 2013)
Department of the Treasury
Internal Revenue Service

**Request for Taxpayer
Identification Number and Certification**

Give Form to
the requester.
Do not send to
the IRS.

Name (as shown on your income tax return)

Business name/disregarded entity name, if different from above

Check appropriate box for federal tax classification:

☑ Individual/sole proprietor   ☐ C Corporation   ☐ S Corporation

☐ Partnership
☐ Trust/estate

☐ Limited liability company.   Enter the tax classification (C=C corporation,
S=S corporation, P=partnership) ►

☐ Other (see instructions) ►

Exemptions (see instructions):

Exempt payee code (if any)____

Exemptions from FATCA reporting code (if any)____

Your name and date will not be in the W9 form yet.

If something is incorrect, click "Previous" to go back and make changes. Otherwise, click the yellow button.

Part II   **Certification**

Under penalties of perjury, I certify that:

1. The number shown on this form is my correct taxpayer identification number (or I am waiting for a number to be issued to me), and

2. I am not subject to backup withholding because: (a) I am exempt from backup withholding, or (b) I have not been notified by the Internal Revenue Service(IRS) that I am subject to backup withholding as a result of a failure to report all interest or dividends, or (c) the IRS has notified me that I am no longer subject to backup withholding, and

3. I am a U.S. citizen or other U.S. person (defined below), and

4. The FATCA code(s) entered on this form (if any) indicating that I am exempt from FATCA reporting is correct.

Signature of U.S. Person :   Date (MM-DD-YYYY) :

STILL REVIEWING, BUT NOTHING TO CLICK HERE EXCEPT THIS

| Exit without saving | | Previous | Save and continue |

You will be brought to this page. Here is how I filled out mine:

Tax Information Interview

Consent to electronic 1099 form

In order for Amazon to provide an electronic version of your tax information reporting Form 1099, the IRS requires that we obtain your consent. If you do not provide consent for electronic delivery of your tax information reporting statements, you may still use the U.S. tax interview process to complete your IRS W-9 or W-8 form. However, at the end of the calendar year, we will mail your completed tax information reporting statements for your records.

If you provide consent for electronic delivery of your tax information reporting statements, you may revoke this consent at any time by retaking the tax information interview.

Note: At this time, not all Amazon businesses have enabled the electronic delivery of Form 1099. You may still receive a paper form from these businesses until the electronic delivery has been enabled.

Electronic 1099 form   ⦿ I consent to electronic receipt of my information reporting documentation
◯ No, mail the documents to me

Consent to electronic signature

In order to electronically sign your tax identity document, it is necessary to obtain your consent. If you do not provide your consent, at the end of the interview you will be required to print the form, sign it with a blue or black pen, and mail it to the address that is provided.

Electronic signature   ⦿ I consent to provide my electronic signature
◯ No, I will mail the documents to you

If you choose Electronic reporting as I did, the page will expand. Enter your name and email address, then click "Submit".

Electronic signature

Under penalties of perjury, I certify that:

☑ The number shown on this form is my correct taxpayer identification number (or I am waiting for a number to be issued to me), and

☑ I am not subject to backup withholding because: (a) I am exempt from backup withholding, or (b) I have not been notified by the Internal Revenue Service (IRS) that I am subject to backup withholding as a result of a failure to report all interest or dividends, or (c) the IRS has notified me that I am no longer subject to backup withholding, and

☑ I am a U.S. citizen or other U.S. person (defined below), and

☑ The FATCA code(s) entered on this form (if any) indicating that I am exempt from FATCA reporting is correct.

The Internal Revenue Service does not require your consent to any provision of this document other than the certifications required to avoid backup withholding.

By typing my name, date, and the e-mail address I use to access my account, I acknowledge I am signing the tax documentation under penalties of perjury.

Signature of U.S. person Type your name	
	! Required
Date mm-dd-yyyy	07-18-2015
E-mail address Email address used to access your account	
	! Required

Once you are satisfied with the information presented in your W-9, and you have signed the certification above, select the Submit button to send your document to Amazon.

Exit without saving	Previous	Submit

You will be brought to the W9 Form again for final review. This time more information will be in the form:

Finally we are finished with the tax information and can proceed with setting up our book. Go ahead and log in:

Sign In

What is your e-mail or mobile number?

E-mail or mobile number: [   ]

Do you have an Amazon.com password?

○ **I am a new customer.**
(you'll create a password later)

◉ **I am a returning customer, and my password is:**

[   ]

[Sign in using our secure server ▶]

Forgot your password?

Setting Up Your First Book

Finally we can setup our first book. After you log in, go to the Bookshelf Page at https://kdp.amazon.com/bookshelf, then click "Add New Title:

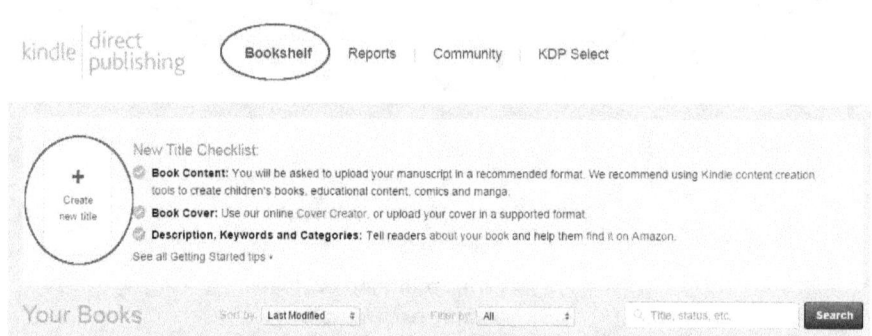

If you have already started setting up your book, you con continue the setup by following the instructions here:

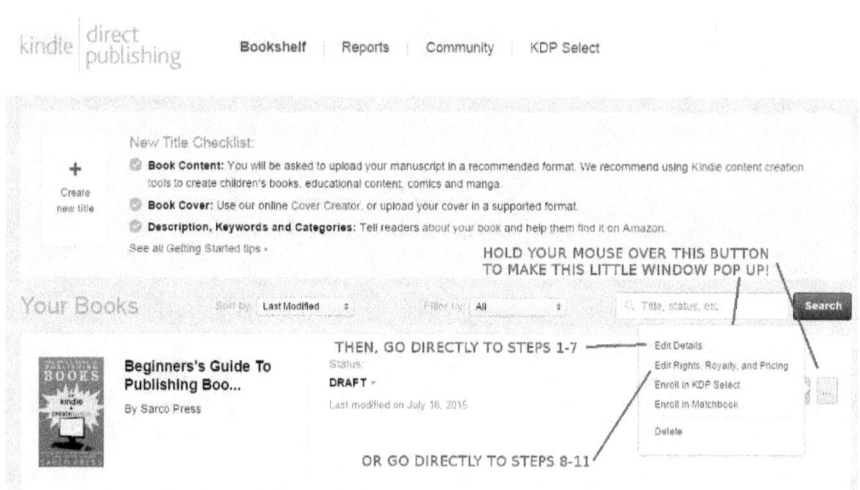

Beginners's Guide To Publishing Books On Kindle and Createspace

Step 1	Step 2	Optional
Your book	**Rights & Pricing**	**KDP Select Benefits**
✓ Complete	i Not Started...	

Introducing KDP Select

Take advantage of KDP Select, an optional program that makes your book exclusive to Kindle and eligible for the following benefits:

- **Reach more readers** - With each 90-day enrollment period, your book will appear in Kindle Unlimited in the U.S., U.K., Italy, Spain, Germany, France, Brazil, Mexico and Canada and the Kindle Owners' Lending Library (KOLL) in the U.S., U.K., Germany, France, and Japan which can help readers discover your book.
- **Earn more money** - Earn your share of the KDP Select Global Fund when customers read your books from Kindle Unlimited and the Kindle Owners' Lending Library. Plus, earn 70% royalty for sales to customers in Japan, India, Brazil and Mexico.
- **Maximize your sales potential** - Choose from two promotional tools including: Kindle Countdown Deals, time-bound promotional discounts for your book, available on Amazon.com and Amazon.co.uk, while earning royalties; or Free Book Promotion, where readers can get your book free for a limited time.

Learn more

NEW AUTHORS SHOULD STRONGLY CONSIDER ENROLLING THE BOOK IN "KINDLE SELECT"

☐ Enroll this book in KDP Select

By checking this box, you are enrolling in KDP Select for 90 days. Books enrolled in KDP Select must not be available in digital format on any other platform during their enrollment. If your book is found to be available elsewhere in digital format, it may not be eligible to remain in the program. See the KDP Select Terms and Conditions and KDP Select FAQs for more information.

Getting Started

Learn more about Kindle content creation tools for children's books, educational content, comics and manga.

1. Enter Your Book Details

ENTER THE BOOK TITLE AND SUBTITLE

Book name

Beginners's Guide To Publishing Books On Kindle and Createspace

Please enter the exact title only. Books submitted with extra words in this field will not be published. (Why?)

Subtitle (optional)

With Dozens of Full Color Images to Show You How It's Done

Please enter the exact subtitle only. Books submitted with extra words in this field will not be published. (Why?)

☐ This book is part of a series (What's this?)

IF THE BOOK IS A SERIES, CHECK THIS BOX AND PUT THE BOOK NUMBER HERE ("1" OR "2" ETC)

Edition number (optional) (What's this?)

Publisher (optional) (What's this?)

OPTIONAL

Sarco Press

Description (What's this?)

THIS IS THE BLURB THAT WILL DISPLAY ON THE AMAZON BOOK PAGE. TAKE SOME TIME AND WRITE A GOOD BLURB THAT WILL ENCOURAGE READERS TO BUY YOUR BOOK!

Do you need to publish your book on Kindle but don't know where to begin?

Maybe you have your book published on Kindle but want to take it to the next level and publish a paperback version?

Book contributors: (What's this?)

CLICK HERE TO ADD YOUR AUTHOR NAME (NOT OPTIONAL)

Sarco Press (Author)

Add contributors

Language (What's this?)

English

ISBN (optional) (What's this?)

IF YOU PURCHASED AN ISBN FROM BOWKER, ENTER IT HERE. OTHERWISE DON'T WORRY ABOUT IT

Steps 2-3

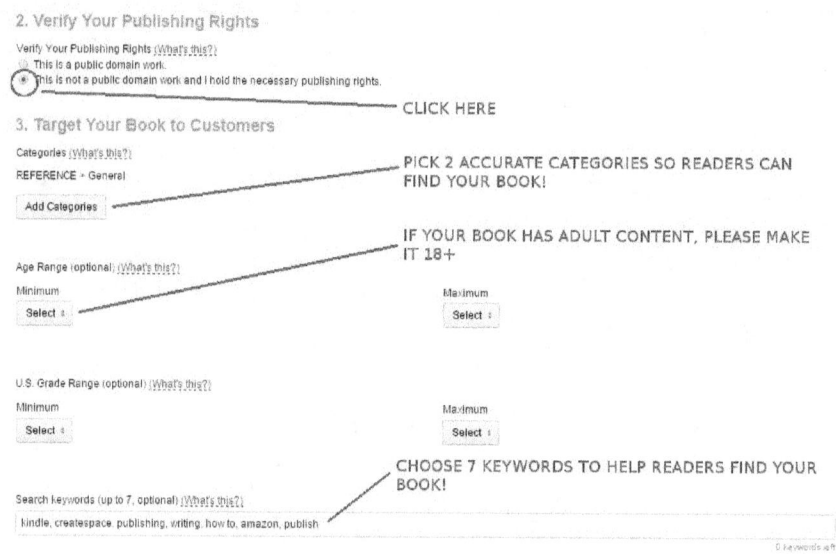

2. Verify Your Publishing Rights

Verify Your Publishing Rights (What's this?)
- This is a public domain work.
- This is not a public domain work and I hold the necessary publishing rights.

⟶ CLICK HERE

3. Target Your Book to Customers

Categories (What's this?)
REFERENCE › General

Add Categories

PICK 2 ACCURATE CATEGORIES SO READERS CAN FIND YOUR BOOK!

IF YOUR BOOK HAS ADULT CONTENT, PLEASE MAKE IT 18+

Age Range (optional) (What's this?)

Minimum
Select ⇕

Maximum
Select ⇕

U.S. Grade Range (optional) (What's this?)

Minimum
Select ⇕

Maximum
Select ⇕

CHOOSE 7 KEYWORDS TO HELP READERS FIND YOUR BOOK!

Search keywords (up to 7, optional) (What's this?)

kindle, createspace, publishing, writing, how to, amazon, publish

0 keywords left

Steps 4-6

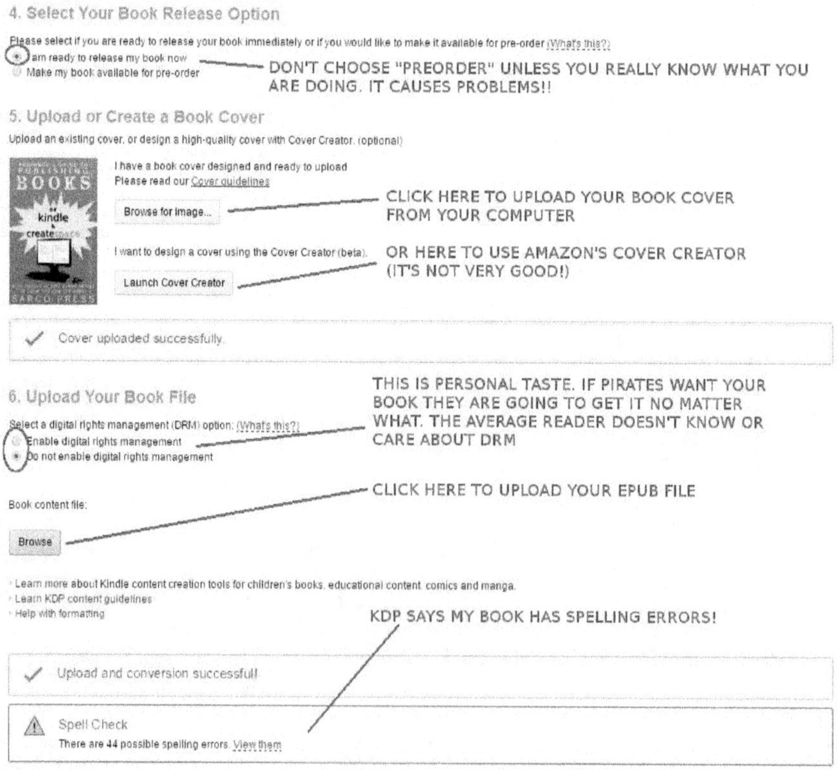

4. Select Your Book Release Option

Please select if you are ready to release your book immediately or if you would like to make it available for pre-order (What's this?)
- I am ready to release my book now
- Make my book available for pre-order

DON'T CHOOSE "PREORDER" UNLESS YOU REALLY KNOW WHAT YOU ARE DOING. IT CAUSES PROBLEMS!!

5. Upload or Create a Book Cover

Upload an existing cover, or design a high-quality cover with Cover Creator. (optional)

I have a book cover designed and ready to upload
Please read our Cover guidelines

Browse for image...

CLICK HERE TO UPLOAD YOUR BOOK COVER FROM YOUR COMPUTER

I want to design a cover using the Cover Creator (beta).

Launch Cover Creator

OR HERE TO USE AMAZON'S COVER CREATOR (IT'S NOT VERY GOOD!)

✓ Cover uploaded successfully.

6. Upload Your Book File

THIS IS PERSONAL TASTE. IF PIRATES WANT YOUR BOOK THEY ARE GOING TO GET IT NO MATTER WHAT. THE AVERAGE READER DOESN'T KNOW OR CARE ABOUT DRM

Select a digital rights management (DRM) option: (What's this?)
- Enable digital rights management
- Do not enable digital rights management

CLICK HERE TO UPLOAD YOUR EPUB FILE

Book content file:

Browse

- Learn more about Kindle content creation tools for children's books, educational content, comics and manga.
- Learn KDP content guidelines
- Help with formatting

KDP SAYS MY BOOK HAS SPELLING ERRORS!

✓ Upload and conversion successful!

⚠ Spell Check
There are 44 possible spelling errors. View them

Step 7

7. Preview Your Book

Previewing your book is an integral part of the publishing process and the best way to guarantee that your readers will have a good experience and see the book you want them to see. KDP offers two options to preview your book depending on your needs. Which should I use?

Online Previewer

THIS IS HOW YOU CAN USE THE ONLINE PREVIEWER AFTER
YOU HAVE UPLOADED YOUR BOOK

For most users, the online previewer is the best and easiest way to preview your content. The online previewer allows you to preview most books as they will appear on Kindle, Kindle Fire, iPad, and iPhone. If your book is fixed layout (for more information on fixed layout, see the Kindle Publishing Guidelines), the online previewer will display your book as it will appear on Kindle Fire.

Preview book

Downloadable Previewer

If you would like to preview your book on Kindle Touch or Kindle DX, you will want to use the downloadable previewer. Instructions

Download Book Preview File

YOU CAN DOWNLOAD THE KDP BOOK HERE TO SEE WHAT IT
LOOKS LIKE AFTER AMAZON CONVERTED IT

Download Previewer: Windows | Mac

Then click the "Save and Continue" button at the bottom left:

Save and Continue   Save as Draft

We are brought to a new page for Step 8:

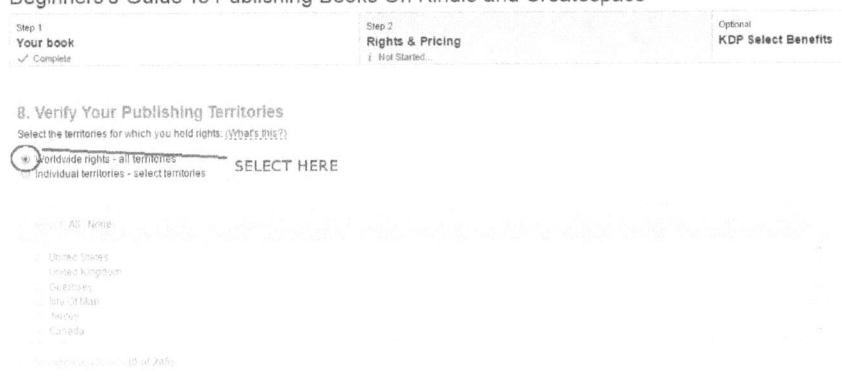

Beginners's Guide To Publishing Books On Kindle and Createspace

Step 1 Your book ✓ Complete	Step 2 Rights & Pricing i Not Started...	Optional KDP Select Benefits

8. Verify Your Publishing Territories

Select the territories for which you hold rights: (What's this?)

- Worldwide rights - all territories   SELECT HERE
- Individual territories - select territories

Select / All / None
- United States
- United Kingdom
- Guernsey
- Isle Of Man
- Jersey
- Canada

Territories are shown (0 of 249)

Step 9, set your selling price:

9. Set Your Pricing and Royalty

KDP Pricing Support (Beta)

See the relationship between price and past sales and author earnings for KDP books like yours.

`View Service` ———————————————— CLICK HERE TO GET AN IDEA OF A PRICE FOR YOUR BOOK

KDP Pricing and Royalty

⚠ Effective January 1, 2015, list prices for EU marketplaces include VAT.
Learn more about VAT

Please select a royalty option for your book. (What's this?)

IF YOUR SELL PRICE IS LESS THAN $2.99 CHOOSE 35%
IF YOUR SELL PRICE IS $2.99 - $9.99 CHOOSE 70%

○ 35% Royalty
● 70% Royalty

ENTER YOUR SELL PRICE HERE
LEAVE THE OTHER FIELDS CHECKED FOR AUTOMATIC

	List Price		Royalty Rate	Delivery Costs	Estimated Royalty
Amazon.com	$ 2.99 USD		35% (Why?)	n/a	$1.05
	Price must be between $2.99 and $9.99		70%	$0.57	$1.69
Amazon.co.uk	☑ Set UK price automatically based on US price £1.99		70%	£0.38	£0.90*
	(£1.66 without UK VAT)				
Amazon.de	☑ Set DE price automatically based on US price €2.99		70%	€0.46	€1.44*
	(€2.51 without DE VAT)				
Amazon.fr	☑ Set FR price automatically based on US price €2.99		70%	€0.46	€1.66*
	(€2.83 without FR VAT)				
Amazon.es	☑ Set ES price automatically based on US price €2.99		70%	€0.46	€1.41*
	(€2.47 without ES VAT)				

And Steps 10-11, the final part:

10. Kindle MatchBook

☑ This title is enrolled in Kindle MatchBook. Uncheck to opt out of the program.

$0.99 ⌄   Estimated royalty: $0.29

IF YOU HAVE A CREATESPACE VERSION OF YOUR BOOK, READERS WHO BOUGHT IT CAN GET A DISCOUNT ON THE KINDLE VERSION IF YOU SELECT THIS

11. Kindle Book Lending

○ Allow lending for this book (Details)

DOES NOT AFFECT AUTHOR'S ROYALTIES WHETHER OR NOT IT IS SELECTED

DON'T FORGET TO CLICK HERE!!

☑ By clicking Save and Publish below, I confirm that I have all rights necessary to make the content I am uploading available for marketing, distribution and sale in each territory I have indicated above, and that I am in compliance with the KDP Terms and Conditions.

<< Back to Your Bookshelf   FINALLY, CLICK HERE TO PUBLISH YOUR BOOK. IT WILL GO "LIVE" AFTER A ——— `Save and Publish` `Save as Draft`
FEW HOURS

Give Amazon a half day or so to finalize everything, and if there are no problems, your book will go "Live" and be available for sale!

But how do we find the book's Amazon page? See below:

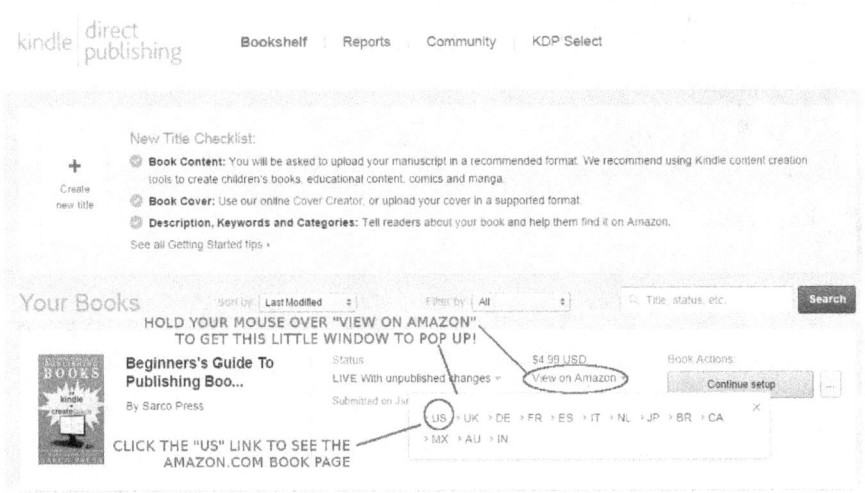

Once your book has gone Live, you can track sales by clicking the "Reports" button on the KDP page:

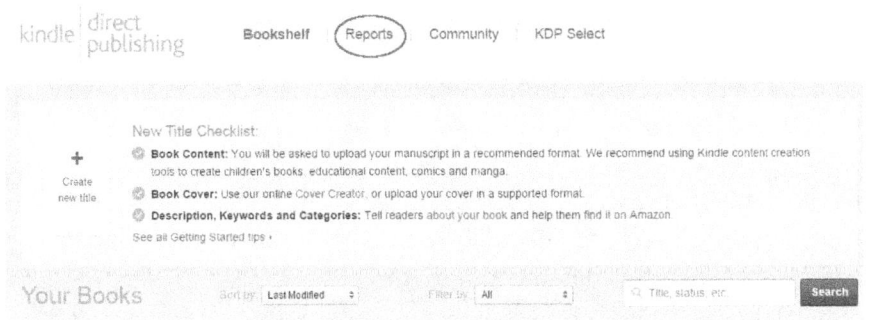

To check the sales ranking of a book you'll have to first go to the book's Amazon page as described above. Then scroll down until you see the "Amazon Best Sellers Rank":

Clark in the Past is a one way time travel trip, adventure and s package. The main character has been flung back thousands the supplies he has with him. Travel along with him as he enc funny and/or deadly.

Kindle Delivers: Daily Deals
Subscribe to find out about each day's Kindle Daily Deal:

Get the Free Kindle App
Enter email or phone number to get a link

Email or mobile number   Send

Product Details

File Size: 380 KB
Print Length: 198 pages
Simultaneous Device Usage: Unlimited
Sold by: Amazon Digital Services, Inc.
Language: English
ASIN: B00Z7LSU7M
Text-to-Speech: Enabled
X-Ray: Not Enabled
Word Wise: Not Enabled
Lending: Enabled
Amazon Best Sellers Rank: #27,435 Paid in Kindle Store (See Top 100 Paid in Kindle Store)
   #72 in Books > Science Fiction & Fantasy > Science Fiction > **Time Travel**
   #99 in Kindle Store > Kindle eBooks > Science Fiction & Fantasy > Science Fiction > **Time Travel**

Would you like to **give feedback on images** or **tell us about a lower price?**

I'm using my friend Scratch's book. It is currently ranked at 27,425. Which is pretty good. There are 8-9 million books on Amazon, and "Clark in the Past" is selling better than most of them.

If no one has bought your book yet, it won't have a ranking. You have to sell at least one book to get a rank.

Now for the bad news! You won't get paid until 60 days after the end of the month that you started selling books! So if you published your first book in mid June, you would get paid for June's royalties at the end of August. After that you will get paid at the end of every month, but the royalties will be for books sold 2 months ago.

Section Two: Createspace

Why Publish Books On Createspace?

For a simple reason: many people like to read real, physical books, not that new-fangled electronic ebook gadget! And ebooks are only a fad! Well, not really, but we'll discuss that later.

Other people like to keep a physical copy of a book they enjoy reading. Maybe it's a non-fiction reference book. People want to leaf through the pages of reference and other non-fiction books.

Another reason people might prefer print books is because, according to Amazon, readers don't really own the kindle books they buy. Readers pay for the right to read the digital form of the book. But Amazon can (and has) taken that right away from purchasers in the past. It doesn't happen often, but it does happen. This leaves some readers leery of paying good money for ebooks.

But a great reason to publish a paperback copy of your book is so that you, the author, can hold it in your hand and leaf through the pages. Trust me, it is a good feeling!

In any case, publishing a paperback on Createspace costs nothing to the author, so there is nothing to lose and everything to gain by publishing in print.

If you want to sell paperback copies of your book on Amazon, you don't deal with Amazon.com at all. Instead Createspace, an Amazon subsidiary, will handle the process of selling your paperback book on Amazon. If you have a Kindle version of the same book on Amazon, your paperback book will be automatically linked to it after a week or so (but only if they have the exact same title!)

Createspace (which is owned by Amazon) is a Print On Demand (PoD) service.

When a reader orders a PoD book, the book is immediately printed with a high-tech printing machine, bound and shipped. There is no worry about inventory because there are no books to store or keep track of until a customer orders one. No worries about your book going out of print (like with a big publishing house) because the book is printed whenever it is ordered.

There is no charge to the author for selling a Createspace PoD book (although Createspace will keep a portion of the selling price – Amazon needs to make money too, after all).

There are at least a few other distributors of "Print On Demand" (PoD) books. Most US authors of PoD books use Createspace (or Lulu), but there are some European PoD distributors as well. The European PoDs don't distribute directly through Amazon, but they may be a better choice if you have European readers because shipping costs may be reduced.

I have formatted a manuscript for a European PoD distributor and the process is not so different from working with a Createspace book. The only hard part (for me) was translating the Swedish instructions for the template.

After you have created your PoD book, you can order single books or cases of books from the distributor for a low price and sell them yourself if you desire. I have done this in the past--it is another avenue to sell your books. You can even sell autographed copies from your web site!

But let's get to the nitty gritty: how to publish your book.

The Bare Minimum You Should Know About Createspace Publishing

If you are sending your book out to be formatted before publishing, here are some important things to know"

Createspace will need a PDF version of your book

The layout and formatting of Word documents can change depending on the PC it is opened on! If I spend hours meticulously formatting a book interior and then send you my masterpiece, it may look jumbled up and sloppy on your PC. This is a common problem and has been addressed by Microsoft. I don't know if Microsoft really knows the cause of the problem, but they do admit things are not rosey.

PDF files, on the other hand, hold their formatting and layout. What I see on my PC is what you will see on your PC, and also what Createspace will see when they print the book.

Make sure your book is proofread and edited

If you think your book might need changes in the text, make sure it's done before having it formatted! Some formatters will make author changes during the formatting process or even after the job is complete, but some won't. And if they are willing to make changes, they may be busy working on other books and will get to your changes when they have time. If the changes are major, it could affect the formatting of the book, requiring even more work and possibly more cost.

3. The Formatter will need some information from you before formatting Can Begin

These include:

The Trim Size. Without the trim size the formatter won't be able to begin working on your book because he won't know what size to make it.

The ISBN Numbers. Without the ISBN Numbers he won't be able to finish the copyright page.

Author name & Full Title. Sometimes these are not evident in the manuscript.

Createspace Publishing Overview

This section will outline the parts of the Createspace publishing process

- Createspace account setup
- Royalty Payment Profile and Payment Information
- Createspace Dashboard and Projects
- Title Information
- ISBN
- Physical Properties (Interior Type, Paper Color, Trim Size)
- PDF Interior File
- Cover
- Cover Finish
- Description and BISAC Category
- Additional Information
- Distribution Channels
- Selling Price

Step By Step Guide to Publishing a Createspace book

Account Setup

Go to Createspace and log in: https://www.createspace.com/:

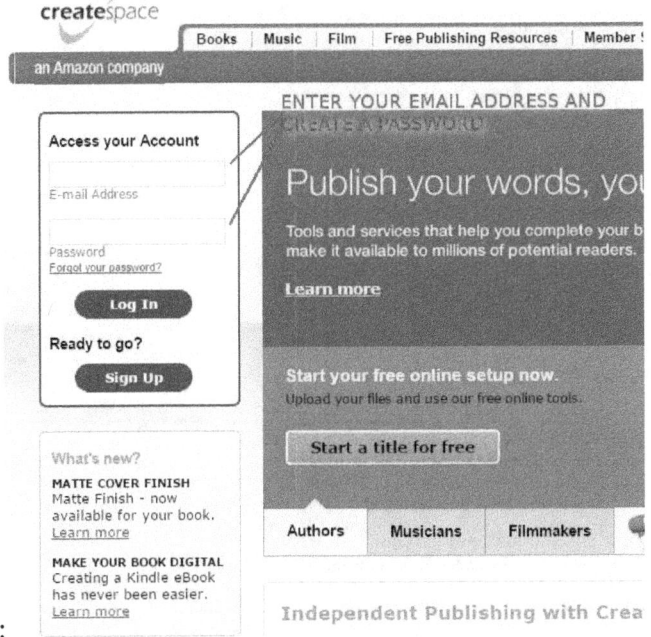

To make a new account go to https://www.createspace.com/Signup.jsp.

Create a New Account

* Email Address

This will be used as your Login ID.

* Password

* Re-Enter

Let's make sure you typed that right.

* First Name

* Last Name

* Country

United States ▼

* What type of media are you considering publishing?

Book ▼

Request a free consultation to learn about our professional fee-based publishing services ☐

Send me Updates and Promotions ☐

We won't sell your contact information. Privacy Policy

Create My Account

Section Two: Createspace

Follow the directions:

Member Agreement
Please read the Membership Agreement contained on this page, and signify you agree to all its terms and conditions using the radio buttons below, then press Continue at the bottom.

Printer friendly version

Last Updated: November 3, 2014

This agreement changed on the date listed above.
See an explanation of the changes at the end of this document.

SERVICES AGREEMENT

This non-exclusive Services Agreement (the "Agreement") contains the complete terms and conditions that apply to your use of the CreateSpace Services (the "Services"), described at https://www.createspace.com/specifications. As used in this Agreement, "we", "our" and "CreateSpace" means, individually:

1. On-Demand Publishing LLC, (a Delaware limited liability Company that does business under the name "CreateSpace"),

2. Amazon Media EU S.à r.l. (a Luxembourg company with its registered office at 5 Rue Plaetis, L-2338, Luxembourg) and/or

3. any other Amazon.com Inc. affiliate that joins as a party to this Agreement as provided in Section 16.

As used in this Agreement, "you" means the person or entity accepting this Agreement. In order to use the Services you must:

1. have registered for an account at our web site, the homepage of which is at www.createspace.com (together with any successor or replacement website, the "Site") by providing your real first and last name, valid address, valid phone number, valid e-mail address and any other required information; and

2. be able to lawfully enter into contracts.

1. Amendment; Notice of Changes

⦿ I agree to all terms and conditions of this Membership Agreement and agree to comply with them at all times.

○ I do not agree to these terms. ——— SELECT "I AGREE"

Continue ——————— THEN CLICK HERE

This window will pop up:

Please Verify Your Email Address

Thanks, your CreateSpace member sign-up is almost complete. Just one more step to get you started.

An email with a confirmation code was sent to   **YOUR EMAIL**   [Resend email]

To verify your email address, be sure to:

Click on the link in the verification email	OR	Enter and verify the confirmation code [Submit]

Check your email:

CreateSpace - Verify Your Email Address

CreateSpace <no_reply@createspace.com>   8:32 PM (0 minutes ago)
to glenn .

Welcome Glenn,
Thanks for signing up with CreateSpace! To activate your account, please verify your email address by clicking on the customized link below:

Click here to get started ——————— CLICK HERE

If you are having trouble with your customized link please visit this page and enter the following code:

RMvB

We appreciate you choosing CreateSpace,
The CreateSpace Team

Please Note: This email was sent from a notification-only address that cannot accept incoming email.

Once you have your Createspace account set up, go to your Createspace Dashboard: https://www.createspace.com/pub/member.dashboard. do

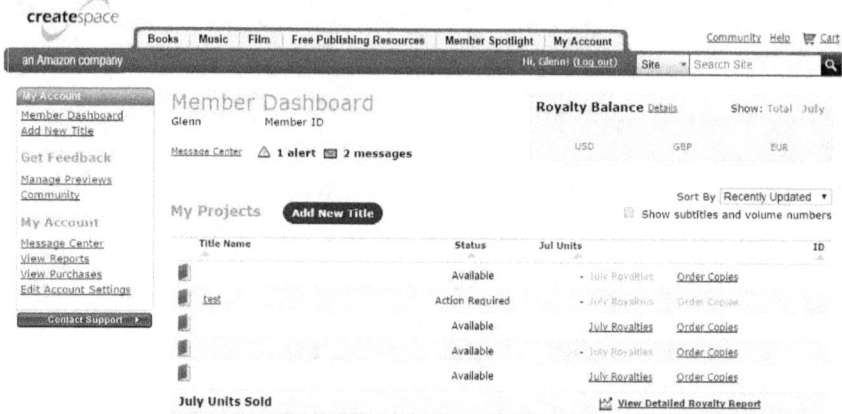

After you have logged into the dashboard, click on **Add New Title** to begin the process of creating your paperback book.

If you've just made your account and verified it through your email, you may be brought to this window:

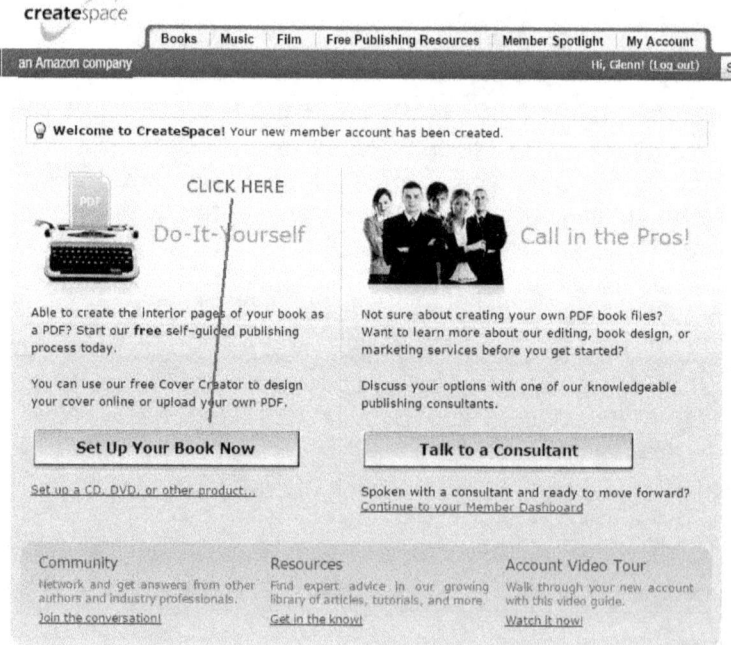

Then enter your title. Make sure it is the exact same title as your Kindle book or the books won't link on Amazon or be sold on the same Amazon page!

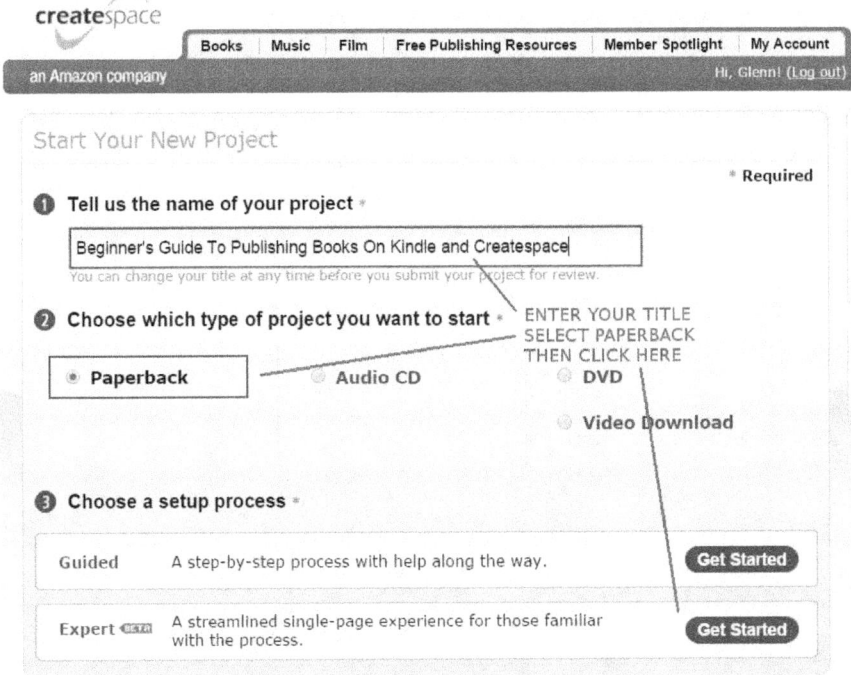

If your Createspace account is new, when you click the "Getting Started" button you'll be brought to the "Missing Royalty Payment Profile" window: Click the link:

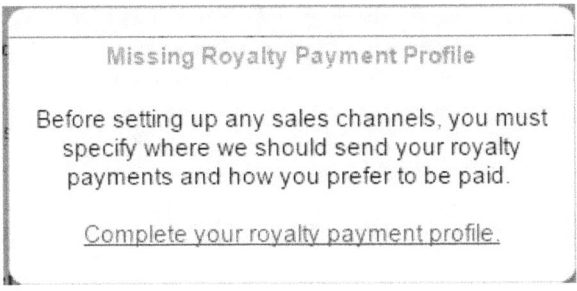

You'll be brought to "Account Settings". Fill everything out:

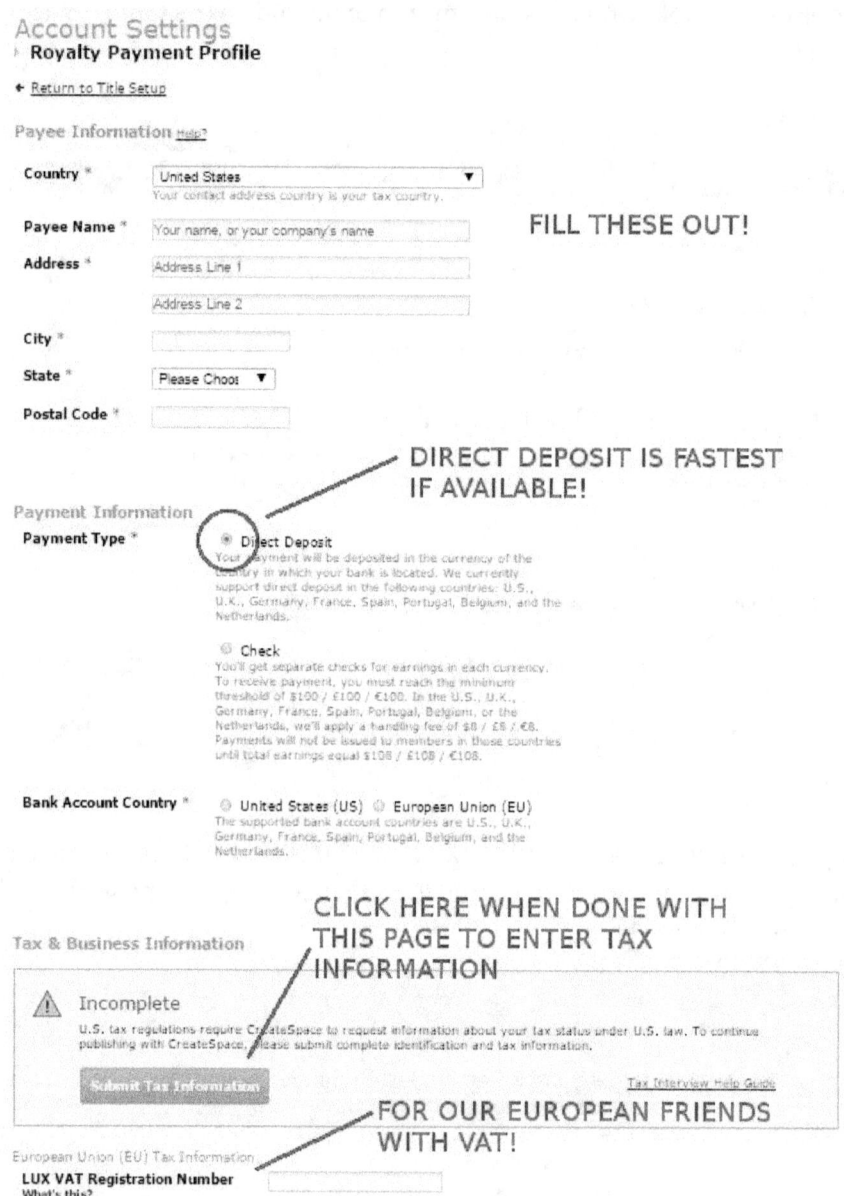

Set up your tax information (it will vary by country) and your royalty payments:

Payment Information

Payment Type *

⦿ Direct Deposit
Your payment will be deposited in the currency of the country in which your bank is located. We currently support direct deposit in the following countries: U.S., U.K., Germany, France, Spain, Portugal, Belgium, and the Netherlands.

○ Check
You'll get separate checks for earnings in each currency. To receive payment, you must reach the minimum threshold of $100 / £100 / €100. In the U.S., U.K., Germany, France, Spain, Portugal, Belgium, or the Netherlands, we'll apply a handling fee of $8 / £8 / €8. Payments will not be issued to members in those countries until total earnings equal $108 / £108 / €108.

Bank Account Country *

⦿ United States (US) ○ European Union (EU)
The supported bank account countries are U.S., U.K., Germany, France, Spain, Portugal, Belgium, and the Netherlands.

Bank Account Number *

Bank Routing Number *

Bank Account Type *   Please Choose ▼

Name on Bank Account *

See these samples to find your Bank Account Number and Bank Routing Number.

Sample Check #1

(⑈9873182 31⑈) (0 111 173632⑈)   236

Sample Check #2

236   (⑈9873182 31⑈) (0 111 173632⑈)

The Bank Routing   The Bank Account
Number is 9 digits   Number is usually
surrounded by ⑈:   left of ⑈

Note: These three sets of numbers may appear in a different order on your check.

Then (finally) you can go back to your "New Project" page and work on entering your book information:

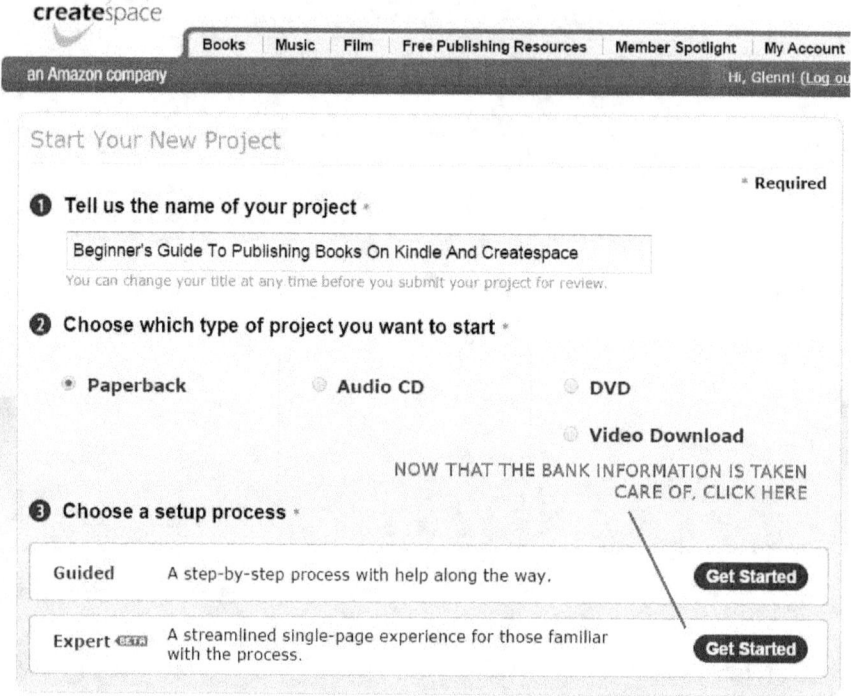

Enter information about the book

This part should be self explanatory. If you're not sure about a title, there is a lot of help on the internet. There are also sites to help you figure out good categories to put your book in, and to write an awesome blurb. If you book isn't in the proper categories, potential readers won't find it. If your blurb is boring, readers won't care when they do find it!

You can change the categories and blurb later, so if you can't think of the perfect categories and blurb right now, just put something in there. But don't forget to make them awesome when you get time!

First let's start with the basics:

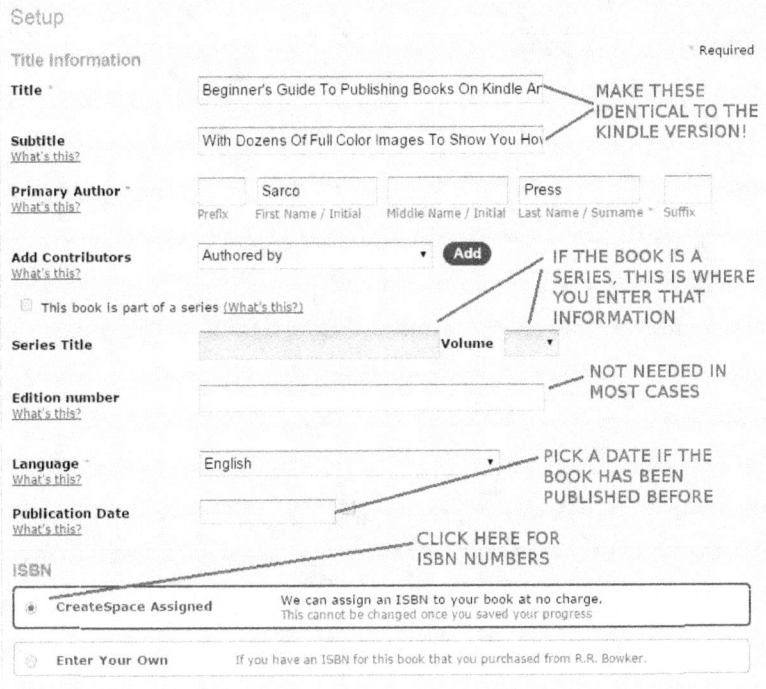

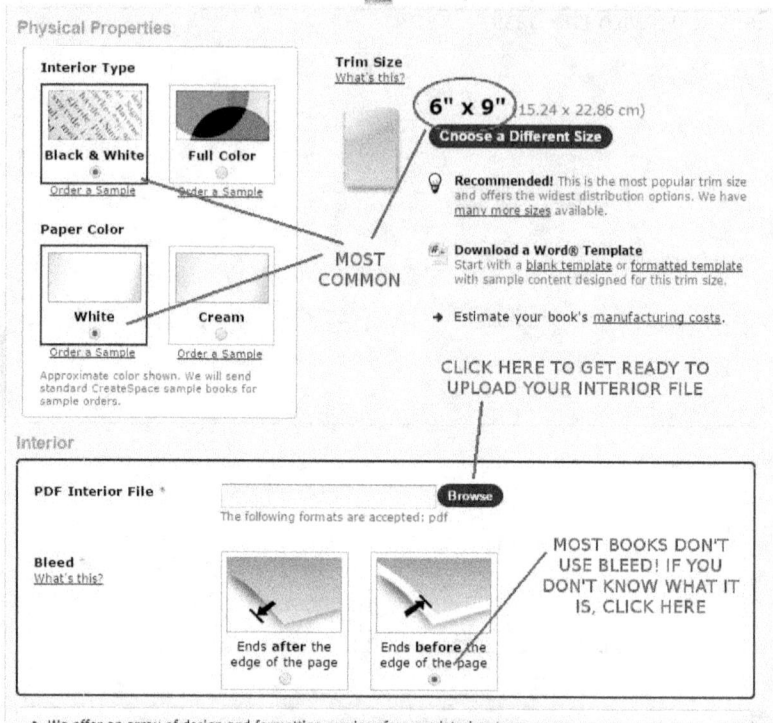

Physical Properties

Interior Type

Black & White
Order a Sample

Full Color
Order a Sample

Paper Color

White
Order a Sample

Cream
Order a Sample

Approximate color shown. We will send standard CreateSpace sample books for sample orders.

MOST COMMON

Trim Size
What's this?

6" x 9" (15.24 x 22.86 cm)
Choose a Different Size

Recommended! This is the most popular trim size and offers the widest distribution options. We have many more sizes available.

Download a Word® Template
Start with a blank template or formatted template with sample content designed for this trim size.

→ Estimate your book's manufacturing costs.

CLICK HERE TO GET READY TO UPLOAD YOUR INTERIOR FILE

Interior

PDF Interior File *   Browse
The following formats are accepted: pdf

Bleed
What's this?

Ends **after** the edge of the page

Ends **before** the edge of the page

MOST BOOKS DON'T USE BLEED! IF YOU DON'T KNOW WHAT IT IS, CLICK HERE

→ We offer an array of design and formatting services for your interior. Learn more

Cover

BUILD YOUR OWN COVER! BETTER THAN THE KINDLE COVER CREATOR

Cover Creator   Launch Cover Creator

PDF Cover File *   Browse
The following formats are accepted: pdf

→ CreateSpace can also provide a variety of cover design services. Learn more

CLICK HERE TO GET READY TO UPLOAD YOUR COVER IF YOU DON'T USE THE COVER CREATOR

Distribute

Cover Finish

Matte   Glossy

I'VE ALWAYS CHOSEN MATTE. IT IS NOT A VITAL DESCISION

Order a Sample   Order a Sample

Note: We'll send standard CreateSpace sample books for sample orders.

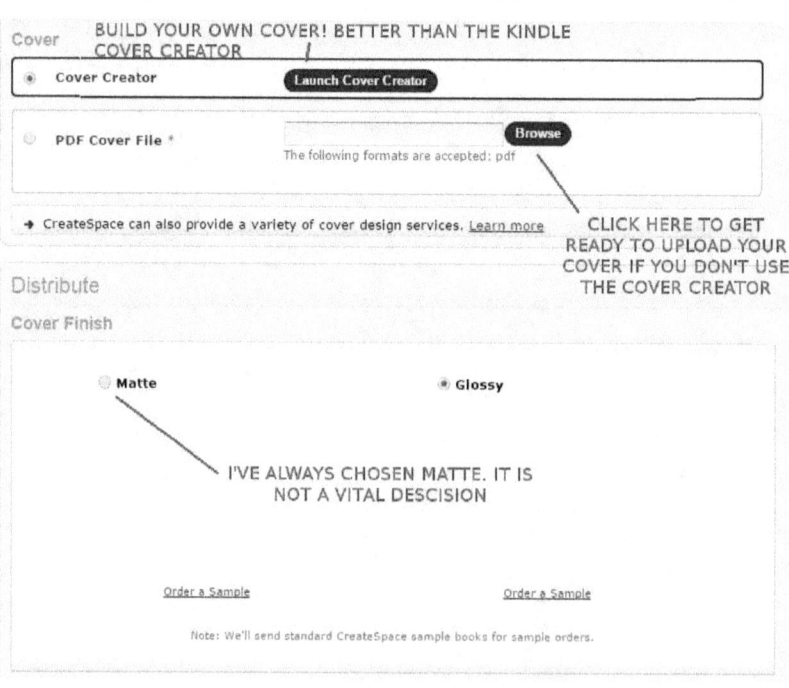

Section Two: Createspace

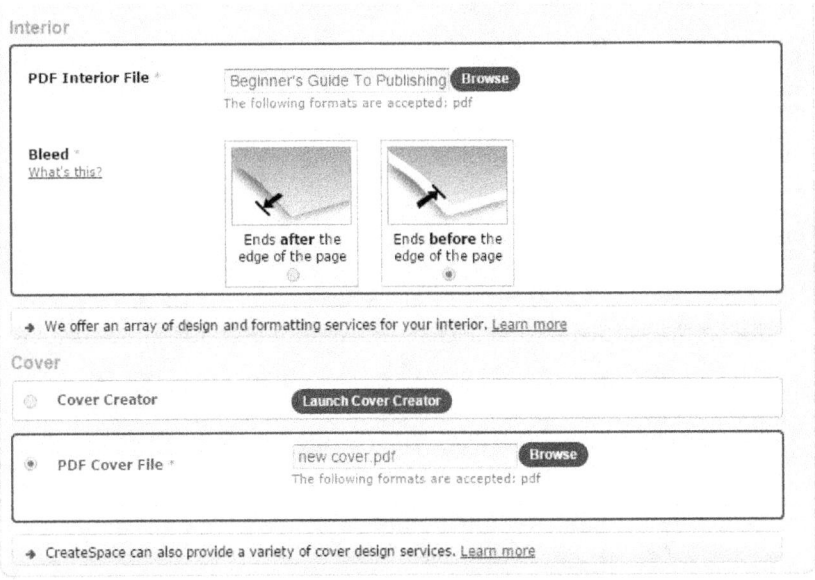

Additional Information (optional)

Author Biography
What's this?   Add

Book Language   English   ▼
What's this?

SAME KEYWORDS AS
KINDLE

Country of Publication   United States   ▼
What's this?

Search Keywords   kindle, createspace, publishing, writing, how to, amazon, pub
What's this?

Contains Adult Content
What's this?

Large Print
What's this?

Then scroll down and save your progress:

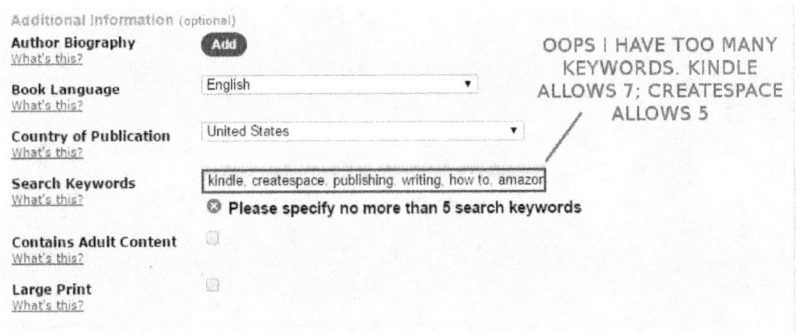

Oops, I've made an error when I copied my keywords from the Kindle version. I'll have to remove some:

Scrolling up the screen shows us that after we saved our progress, we obtained our ISBNs. Copy and paste these somewhere so they can be put on your book's copyright page by the formatter:

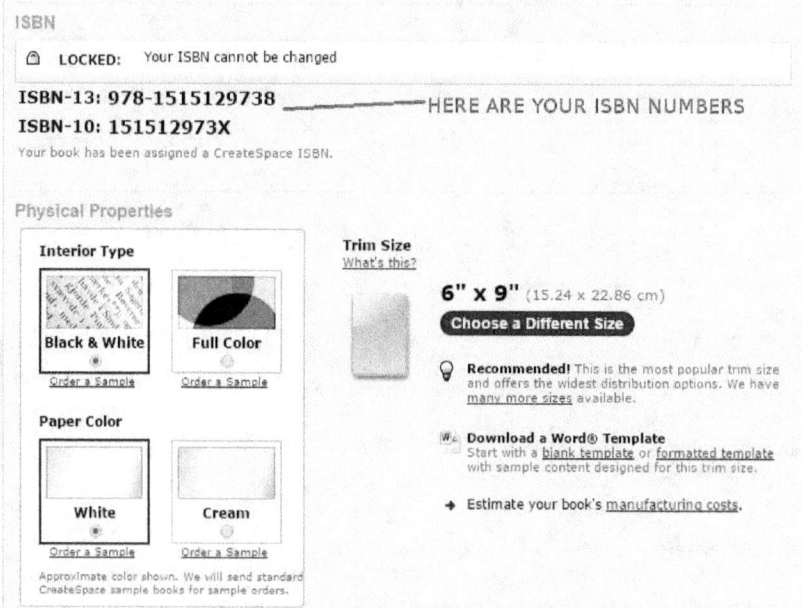

Let's say that my Interior and my Cover are ready for upload. I clicked the "Browse" buttons and showed Createspace where my files are, but they won't upload until I click "Save Progress" at the bottom. Note that uploading the files doesn't have to be done now!

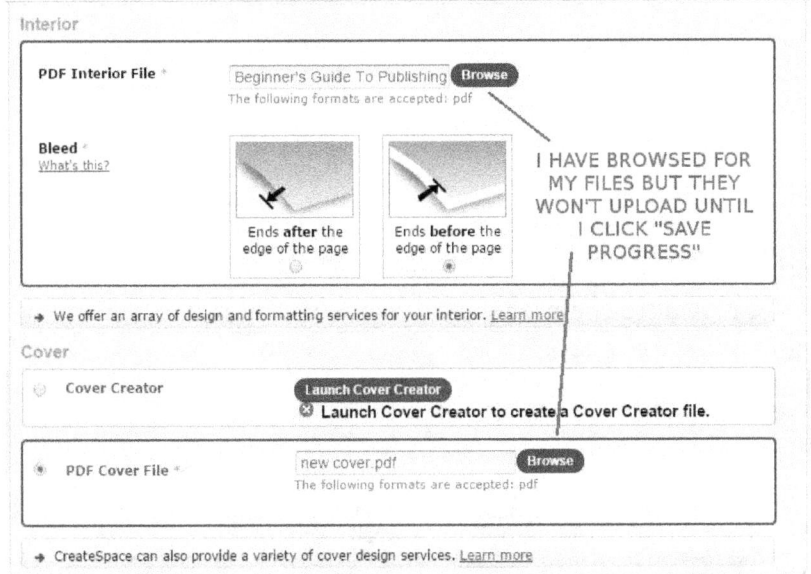

Then click "Save Progress" yet again:

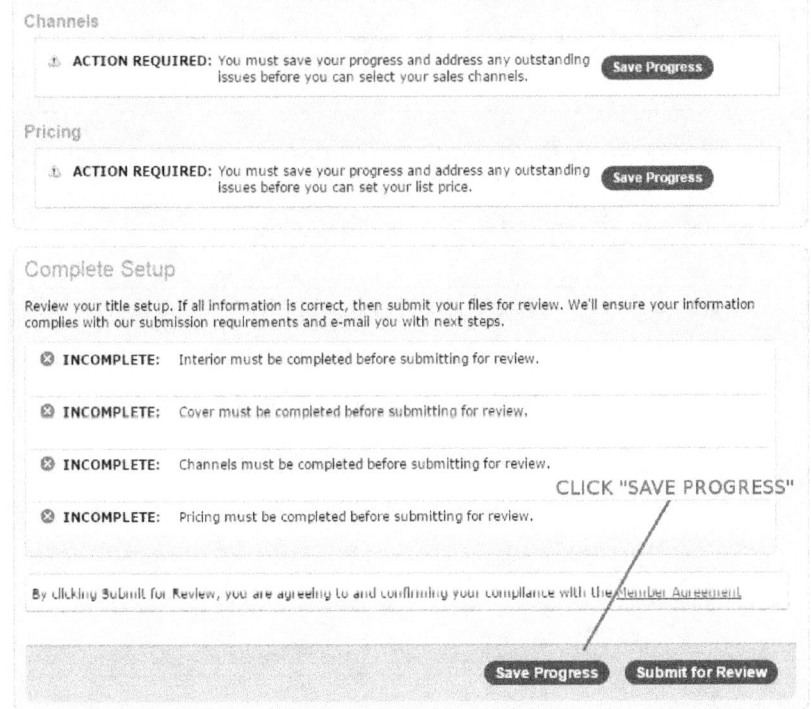

Then wait while the Interior and Cover files upload to Createspace from your computer:

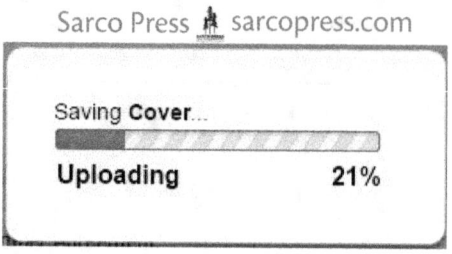

Saving **Cover**...

Uploading   **21%**

We are almost to the end!

We are moved to the next screen where we can pick our distribution channels to sell our book:

Channels

Standard Distribution FREE

SELECT EVERYTHING! (WHY NOT?)

✓ Selected → **a** **Amazon.com**
What's this?

✓ Selected → **a** **Amazon Europe**
What's this?

✓ Selected → **CreateSpace eStore**
What's this?

→ eStore Setup   → Discount Codes

Expanded Distribution FREE

✓ Selected → **Bookstores and Online Retailers**
What's this?

✓ Selected → **Libraries & Academic Institutions**
What's this?

✓ Selected → **CreateSpace Direct**
What's this?

Then we enter our selling price:

Then click "Save Progress" for the last time, and then "Submit For Review":

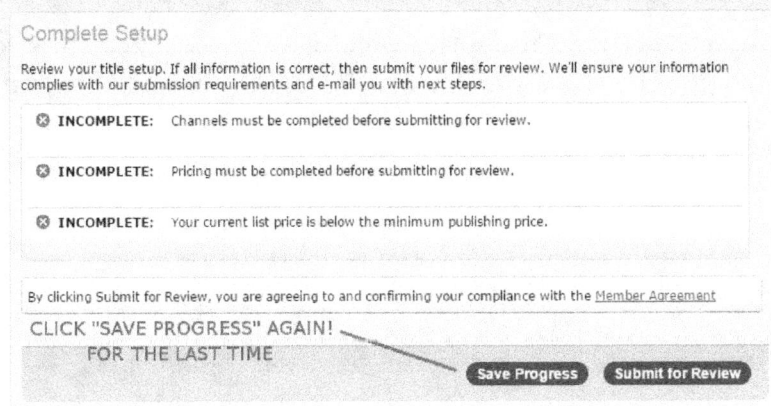

Then we are brought to our book's Project Page:

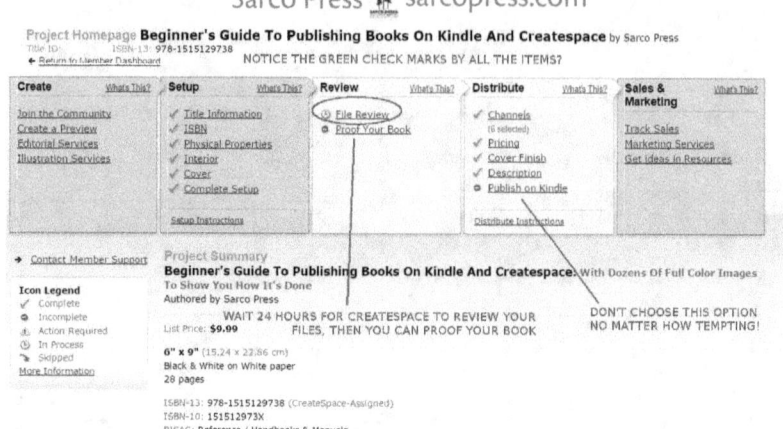

And that's it! After a day or so, Createspace will let us know if there is a problem with either the Interior File or the Cover File, and we can view the digital proofs.

It is advised to order one physical proof through the mail to check for printing errors. The purpose of the proof is not to proofread your book for spelling and grammar errors! That should have been done before your book was formatted!

The purpose of the Createspace proof is to check that all the fonts printed properly and within the margins and the images (if any) are of high enough quality.

More About Createspace Publishing

The Interior File

The Interior part of your book is everything between the front cover and the back cover; essentially your formatted manuscript. The de facto guide for formatting the interior of a physical book is the Chicago Manual of Style, and this is the reference that I and most other professional Book Formatters use when formatting print books.

When the author is setting up the book in the Createspace Project Homepage, there are two important criteria that are important to the Book Formatter and the Cover Designer: the Trim Size and the Paper Type.

Get your ISBN numbers for the book

As a Book Formatter, I like to put the ISBN Numbers in the copyright page. It makes for a more professional book. But I need to get those numbers from the author.

After you have entered your Title Information, navigate to the ISBN section of the Project Homepage. This is where you can enter ISBN numbers for your book or have Createspace generate them. To find out more about ISBN numbers go to **http://www.isbn.org/**. But I'll just say that at least one ISBN number is necessary to publish your book.

You can't arbitrarily assign ISBN numbers. They must either be purchased through an agency or assigned by Createspace. Most Createspace authors just go with whatever ISBN numbers Createspace assigns. I don't know of any reason not to do this.

If you prefer, you can purchase and enter your own ISBN number. ISBN numbers for U.S. books can be purchased from Bowker at **http://www. isbn.org/**. They are expensive. If you use the Createspace assigned ISBN numbers, you will have full rights to your work. I'll say it again, *Createspace will not own your work if you use their ISBN numbers!* Createspace is the "printer" of your work, not the "publisher". The author is the publisher and retains all rights to the work, unless the author has made an agreement with a third-party publishing company.

There are two Createspace ISBN numbers: a thirteen digit number and a ten digit number. I usually put them in the copyright page. Here is what one of my own copyright pages looks like:

SARCO
PRESS

Copyright © 2015 Sarco Press

ISBN-13: 978-1506155951
ISBN-10: 1506155952

Note that the logo is my company publishing logo and you won't have it on your copyright page. If you don't have a custom copyright page or a logo, your copyright page may look like this:

Copyright © 2015 Author Name

ISBN-13: XXX-XXXXXXXXXX
ISBN-10: XXXXXXXXXX

Obviously your name will be where it says "Author Name"!

If you want to make a fancy copyright page with a logo, mine might give you some ideas, but it's not necessary. If you have a custom copyright text and/or a copyright logo, let the Book Formatter know and he can put them in the book!

It is not required to put the ISBN numbers in the copyright page, but it produces a more professional looking book.

Trim Size

Fifty years ago the trim size of a book might have made a difference in whether or not the book sells to readers. Currently there are both fiction and nonfiction books available in all trim sizes. Most non-fiction books (and many fiction books) use a trim size of 6"x9" (and that happens to be the size of this book), but nonfiction workbooks may be better with a larger trim size. Many novels are formatted in 5.25"x 8" or 5.5"x8.5". For more information about Createspace trim sizes go **here**.

Just make sure to pick an **industry standard trim size** to save on printing costs. Also keep in mind that the more pages your book has, the more it will cost to print and the less you will make in royalties. It is better for your pocketbook to go with a trim size of 6"x9" and 250 pages than 5.5"x8.5" and 350 pages. To calculate your royalties with different trim sizes and page numbers, **go here** and click on the *Royalties* tab, then scroll down.

Paper Type

There are two paper types; **white or cream**. Neither choice affects the interior format of the book, but this information will be important to the **Cover Designer** because cream paper is thicker and makes the spine wider.

Color verses Black and White Printing

Covers are always printed in color, but you must choose whether your Interior is printed in color or black and white.

Book interiors printed in color are more attractive but they cost a lot more to print, meaning the author gets less money in her pocket. For example, using the Createspace **Royalty Calculator**, I find that if I sell a 6x9 book printed in B&W with 250 pages and price it at $10.00, my royalties will be $2.15.

But if I choose color printing for that same book and sell it for the same price, my royalties will be -$12.35. What does this mean? Playing with the royalty calculator I see that to sell the same book in color I need to charge $30.59 *just to break even*. And few people will pay over thirty dollars for a book!

Remember, if you thought about colored formatting for the interior of you book but you choose B&W printing, all the colors will come out in varying shades of gray!

Images

Images for color printing should be **at least 300 dpi** and images for black and white printing should be **at least 600 dpi**. These are Createspace recommendations, but they will print images with a very low resolution if you wish.

Personally, I have published a Createspace book with dozens of color photographs but the book is printed in B&W. The majority of the images are 300 dpi, but some of them were less. After I uploaded the book, I got some Createspace red flags and recommendations to use higher resolution images, but Createspace did accept the upload. I ordered a proof copy and the photos look acceptable. But use at least 300 dpi images if you can.

I've found that by tweaking the contrast and brightness of color images they look much better when printed in B&W. If you plan to do this, you should do it before you send the manuscript to the Book Formatter, or be prepared to pay extra for her to do it for you.

Page Bleed

Basically, bleed is when graphics extend all the way to the edge of the paper and is used for graphics intensive books with a strong visual feature. Most authors don't need to use bleed.

{need more information}

Cover Choices

Cover choices are glossy and matte, and are personal taste. I've used matte and find that it is fine, but I haven't tried glossy yet.

{need more information}

Interior Uploading

After formatting the author's Interior, the Book Formatter will produce a file ready for upload to Createspace. The uploadable file will be in **Portable Document Format (PDF)**. The author should review the PDF file before uploading to Createspace. For this job some authors use **Adobe Acrobat Reader DC**, but there are other free options available. For quick PDF viewing without installing a large program, I find that **Foxit Reader** is my go-to favorite. It's light and fast and doesn't take up hundreds of megabytes of hard drive space like Adobe's bloated Acrobat.

The author should check for errors and offer input to the Book Formatter for any changes requested. In my Book Designing gigs I usually offer free unlimited revisions, so the author can relax knowing she is not under a time constraint to get the formatting correct. But I understand that authors want to get their work published as soon as possible. I try to answer all requests within a few hours at most.

After the job has been accepted and paid for, the author and I sometimes continue to edit the file for days or weeks afterward, up until the author has ordered and received a physical book from Createspace, proofed it and is satisfied!

The Cover File

When setting up how the interior of your book will be printed, you will have a choice of paper type. Paper types include white and cream. Which type you pick is up to you, but your **Cover Designer** will need to know. Cream paper is thicker and changes the width of the books spine. That's why a professional cover formatter can't setup the cover until he or she has the page count and the paper type!

The Interior file should be uploaded before the cover file because the number of pages in the interior will determine the thickness of the spine. Your Cover file won't be approved by Createspace unless it will fit properly on the book.

That's why the cover formatter needs to know the number of pages in the book and the paper type.

Createspace will take a day or two to approve your Interior and Cover. Then your book will go on sale at Amazon. It won't show up there right away; it might take as long as a week. Then you can watch your book sell to readers!

Page Bleed

Basically, bleed is when graphics extend all the way to the edge of the paper and is used for graphics intensive books with a strong visual feature. Most authors don't need to use bleed.

About the Author

I'm a former adventurer and have traveled the world. I've lived in big cities both in the US and abroad, but the calling of the peace and quiet of nature drew me to the mountains of Montana. I live with my family off the grid, in a house we built with our own hands. We raise some livestock and grow some of our own food and live in harmony with the wild beasts of the forest. I wouldn't have it any other way.

I'm a proud descendant of the Amish, and my life is an odd juxtaposition of cutting edge technology and old fashioned living.

I do all my book formatting work on a dual monitor PC powered with solar energy and my internet connection is over my Android cell phone. When I'm not formatting books for clients I'm writing my own books or repairing the tractor, feeding the chickens, improving the house, walking through the woods with the dogs (and goats!) or working on my sawmill.

I'm a published author and wrote a book about my homesteading adventure:

My author web page is here: gordonblaine.com

Thanks for reading!

Why Should You Pick Me To Format Your Book?

Formatting Interiors for Createspace and ebooks is hard work. I've spent years perfecting my craft, but more importantly, I am a published author myself. So I know how it is.

I get it. Your book is your baby, and it needs to be perfect. Maybe you have an idea you'd like to implement in the formatting, or maybe you'd rather I implement my own creative decisions and let you take it from there.

Either way is fine with me! I'm here to help you get what you need and we'll work together.

Print and Ebook Formatting Services

I specialize in making professional fiction or non-fiction books with tables and/or graphics!

I can take a roughly formatted Word Document and make a beautiful print book! Front matter and back matter w/ separate page numbers, TOC, footers, headers.

Standard paragraph indentation; drop caps for fiction & any special formatting you need. If you're not sure how much it should cost, send me the manuscript (or sample) and I'll give a fair, binding quote.

I will deliver a pdf file and/or an epub file with free unlimited formatting revisions until you order your proof!

A fiction work usually costs $40 for either Createspace or ebook versions, or $60 for both.

All my customers have been extremely pleased! I know you're very picky about your book. It's your baby, you should be! If you aren't sure how to go about this, I can guide you or do it for you.

I'll make a copyright page for you if you don't have specific requirements.

I have samples on the web site to help decide on layouts and fonts.

If I format both your Createspace book and your ebook, I'll format your existing cover for free!

If you have questions, email me at glenn@sarcopress.com

www.ingramcontent.com/pod-product-compliance
Lightning Source LLC
Chambersburg PA
CBHW070316290526
45791CB00003B/1129